The Moon is Earth's only proper natural satellite. At one-quarter the diameter of Earth (comparable to the width of Australia), it is the largest natural satellite in the Solar System relative to the size of its planet, and the fifth largest satellite in the Solar System overall (larger than any dwarf planet). Orbiting Earth at an average *lunar distance* of 384,400 km (238,900 mi), or about 30 times Earth's diameter, its gravitational influence is the main driver of Earth's tides and slightly lengthens Earth's day. The Moon is classified as a planetary-mass object and a differentiated rocky body, and lacks any significant atmosphere, hydrosphere, or magnetic field. Its surface gravity is about one-sixth of Earth's (0.1654 g); Jupiter's moon is the only satellite in the Solar System known to have a higher surface gravity and density.

The Moon's orbit around Earth has a sidereal period of 27.3 days, and a synodic period of 29.5 days. The synodic period drives its lunar phases, which form the basis for the months of a lunar calendar. The Moon is tidally locked to Earth, which means that the length of a full rotation of the Moon on its own axis (a lunar day) is the same as the synodic period, resulting in its same side (the near side) always facing Earth.

The near side of the Moon is marked by dark volcanic maria ("seas"), which fill the spaces between bright ancient crustal highlands and prominent impact craters. The lunar surface is relatively non-reflective, with a reflectance just slightly brighter than that of worn asphalt. However, because it reflects direct sunlight, is contrasted by the relatively dark sky, and has a large apparent size when viewed from Earth, the Moon is the brightest celestial object in Earth's sky after the Sun.

The first manmade object to reach the Moon was the Soviet Union's Luna 2 uncrewed spacecraft in 1959; this was followed by the first successful soft landing by Luna 9 in 1966. The only human lunar missions to date have been those of the United States' NASA Apollo program, which conducted the first manned lunar orbiting mission with Apollo 8 in 1968. Beginning with Apollo 11, six human landings took place between 1969 and 1972.

These and later uncrewed missions returned lunar rocks which have been used to develop a detailed geological understanding of the Moon's origins, internal structure, and subsequent history; the most widely accepted origin explanation posits that the Moon formed about 4.51 billion years ago, not long after Earth, out of the debris from a giant impact between the planet and a hypothesized Mars-sized body called Theia.

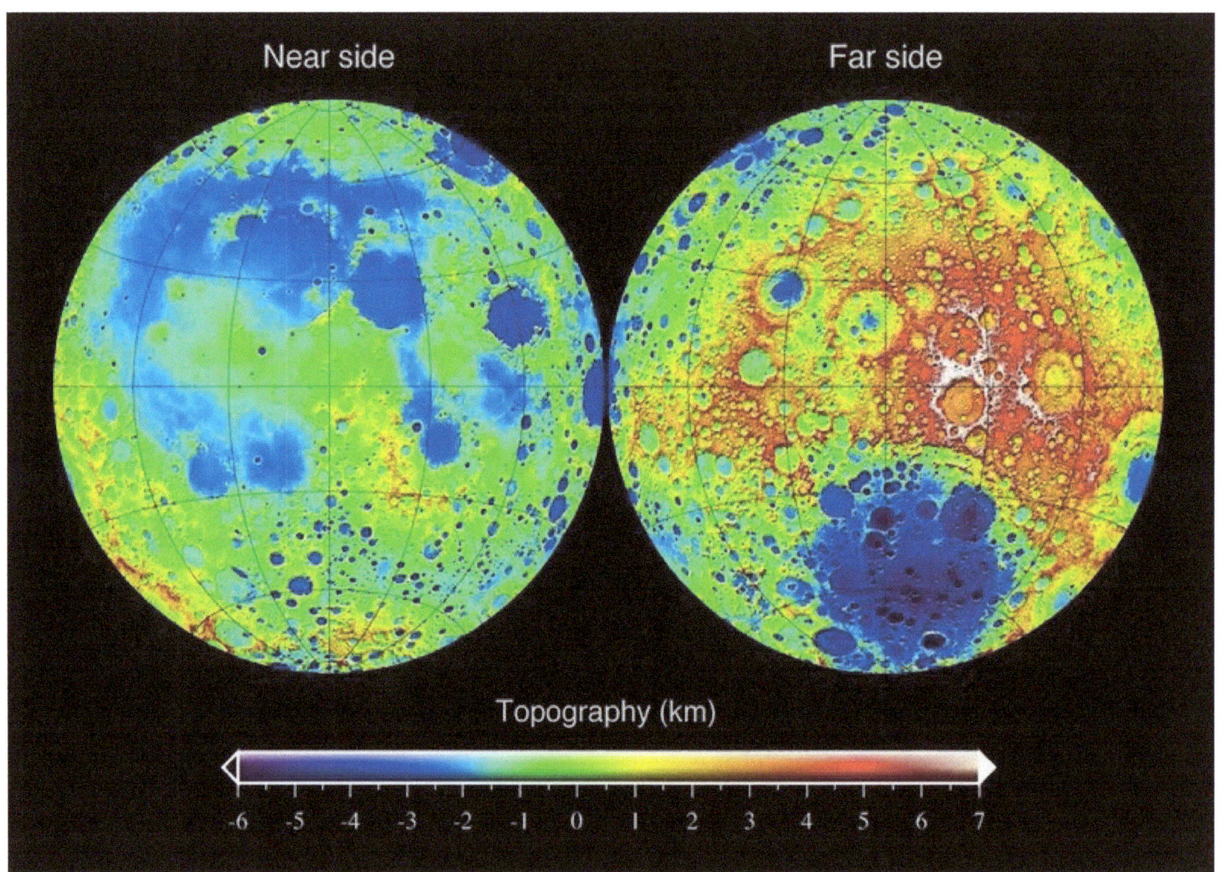

Both the Moon's natural prominence in the earthly sky and its regular cycle of phases as seen from Earth have provided cultural references and influences for human societies and cultures throughout history. Such cultural influences can be found in language, calendar systems, art, and mythology.

Name and etymology

The usual English proper name for Earth's natural satellite is simply the Moon, with a capital M. The noun *moon* is derived from Old English *mōna*, which (like all

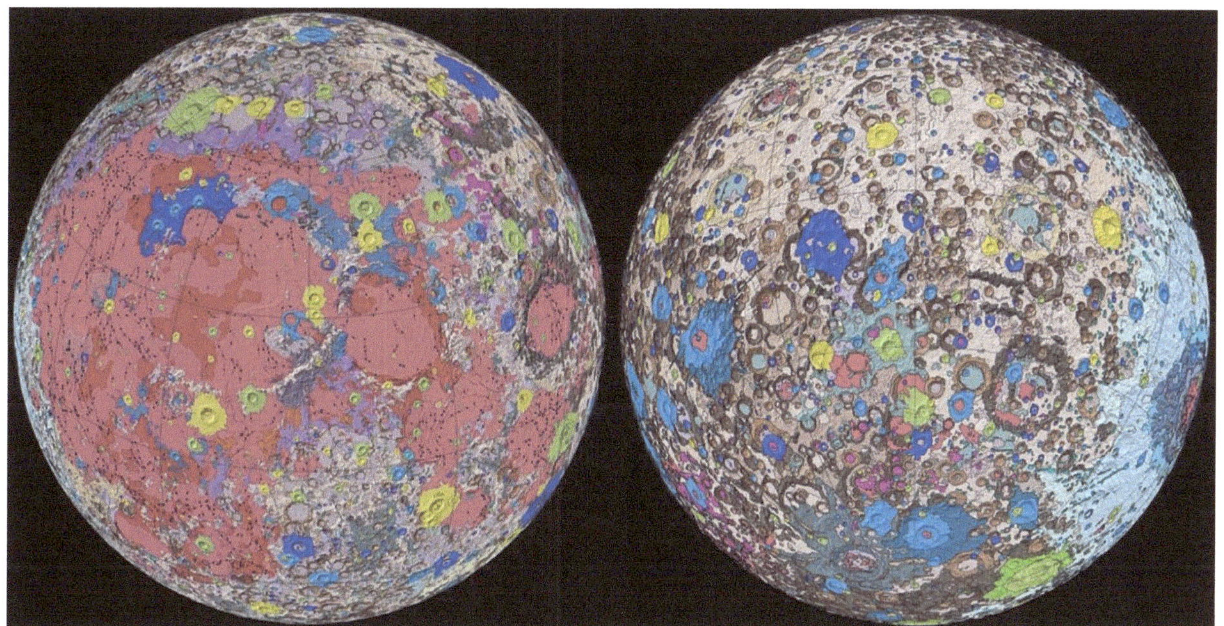

its Germanic cognates) stems from Proto-Germanic *mēnōn*, which in turn comes from Proto-Indo-European *mēnsis* "month (from earlier *mēnōt*, genitive *mēneses*) which may be related to the verb "measure" (of time).

The usual English adjective pertaining to the Moon is "lunar", derived from the Latin word for the Moon, *lūna*. The adjective *selenian* derived from the Greek word for the Moon, and used to describe the Moon as a world rather than as an object in the sky, is rare, while its cognate *selenic* was originally a rare synonym but now nearly always refers to the chemical element selenium. The Greek word for the Moon does however provide us with the prefix *seleno-*, as in *selenography*, the study of the physical features of the Moon, as well as the element name *selenium*.

The Greek goddess of the wilderness and the hunt, Artemis, equated with the Roman Diana, one of whose symbols was the Moon and who was often regarded as the goddess of the Moon, was also called Cynthia, from her legendary birthplace on Mount Cynthus.

Formation

The Moon formed 4.51 billion years ago, or even 100 million years earlier, some 50 million years after the origin of the Solar System, as research published in 2019 suggests. Several forming mechanisms have been proposed, including the fission of the Moon from Earth's crust

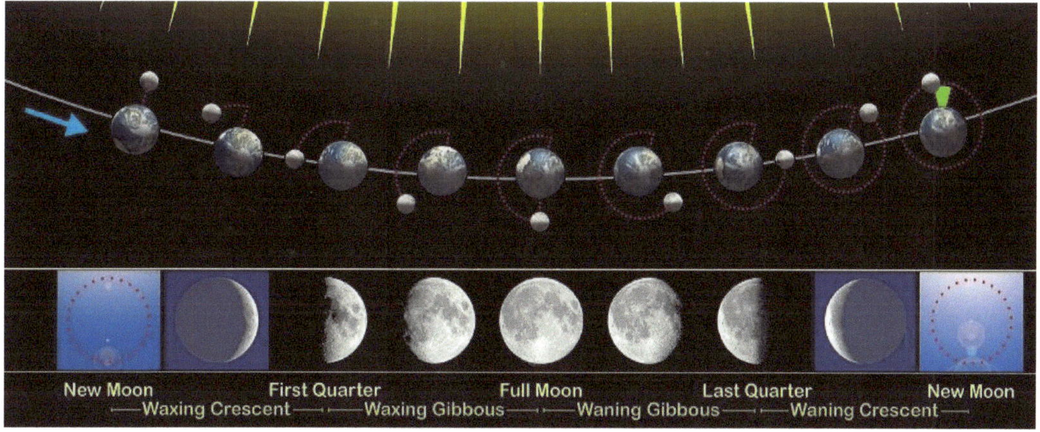

through centrifugal force (which would require too great an initial rotation rate of Earth), the gravitational capture of a pre-formed Moon (which would require an unfeasibly extended atmosphere of Earth to dissipate the energy of the passing Moon), and the co-formation of Earth and the Moon together in the primordial accretion disk (which does not explain the depletion of metals in the Moon).

The prevailing theory is that the Earth–Moon system formed after a giant impact of a Mars-sized body (named *Theia*) with the proto-Earth. The impact blasted material into Earth's orbit and then the material accreted and formed the Moon.

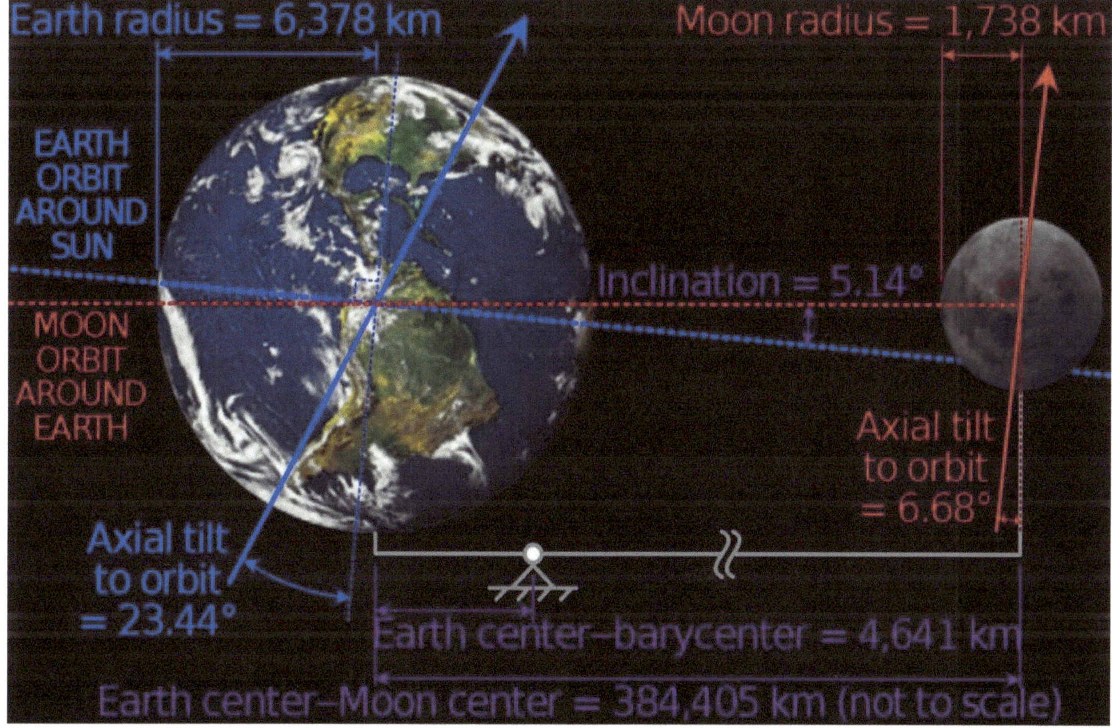

This theory best explains the evidence. Eighteen months prior to an October 1984 conference on lunar origins, Bill Hartmann, Roger Phillips, and Jeff Taylor challenged fellow lunar scientists: "You have eighteen months. Go back to your Apollo data, go back to your computer, do whatever you have to, but make up your mind. Don't come to our conference unless you have something to say about the Moon's birth." At the 1984 conference at Kona, Hawaii, the giant-impact hypothesis emerged as the most consensual.

These simulations also show that most of the Moon derived from the impactor, rather than the proto-Earth. However, more recent simulations suggest a larger fraction of the Moon derived from the proto-Earth. Other bodies of the inner Solar System such as Mars and Vesta have, according to meteorites from them, very different oxygen and tungsten isotopic compositions compared to Earth.

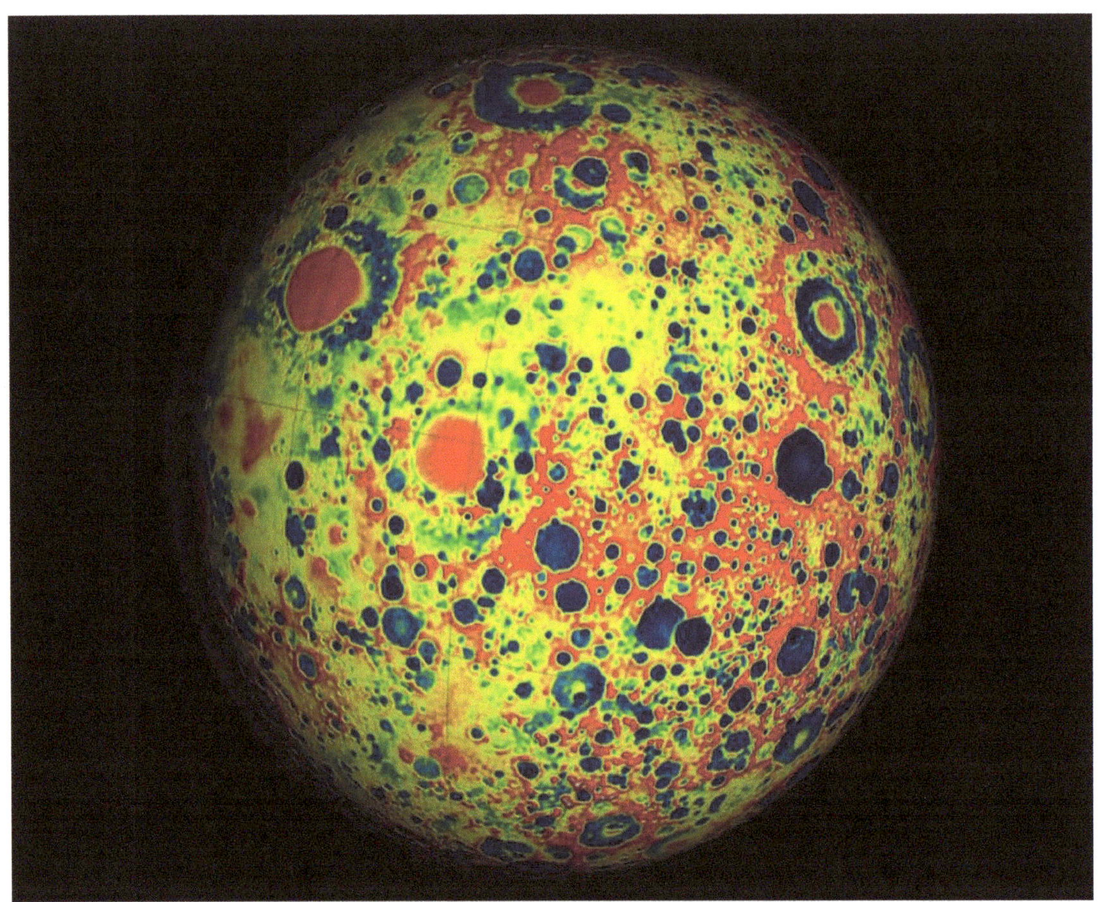

However, Earth and the Moon have nearly identical isotopic compositions. The isotopic equalization of the Earth-Moon system might be explained by the post-impact mixing of the vaporized material that formed the two, although this is debated.
The impact released a lot of energy and then the released material re-accreted into the Earth–Moon system. This would have melted the outer shell of Earth, and thus

formed a magma ocean. Similarly, the newly formed Moon would also have been affected and had its own lunar magma ocean; its depth is estimated from about 500 km (300 miles) to 1,737 km (1,079 miles).

In 2001, a team at the Carnegie Institute of Washington reported the most precise measurement of the isotopic signatures of lunar rocks. The rocks from the Apollo program had the same isotopic signature as rocks from Earth, differing from almost all other bodies in the Solar System. This observation was unexpected, because most of the material that formed the Moon was thought to come from Theia and it was announced in 2007 that there was less than a 1% chance that Theia and Earth had identical isotopic signatures. Other Apollo lunar samples had in 2012 the same titanium isotopes composition as Earth, which conflicts with what is expected if the Moon formed far from Earth or is derived from Theia.

Physical characteristics

Mean radius	1737.4 km (0.2727 of Earth's)
Equatorial radius	1738.1 km (0.2725 of Earth's)
Polar radius	1736.0 km (0.2731 of Earth's)
Flattening	0.0012
Circumference	10921 km (equatorial)
Surface area	3.793×10^7 km^2 (0.074 of Earth's)
Volume	2.1958×10^{10} km^3 (0.020 of Earth's)
Mass	7.342×10^{22} kg (0.012300 of Earth's)

Mean density	3.344 g/cm^3 0.606 × Earth	
Surface gravity	1.62 m/s^2 (0.1654 g)	
Moment of inertia factor	0.3929±0.0009	
Escape velocity	**2.38 km/s** **(8600 km/h; 5300 mph)**	
Sidereal rotation period	27.321661 d (synchronous)	
Equatorial rotation velocity	4.627 m/s	
Axial tilt	• 1.5424° to ecliptic • 6.687° to orbit plane[2] • 24° to Earth's equator	
North pole right ascension	• 17^h 47^m 26^s • 266.86°	
North pole declination	65.64°	
Albedo	**0.136**	

Surface temp.	min	mean	max
Equator	100 K	250 K	390 K
85°N		150 K	230 K

Apparent magnitude	• −2.5 to −12.9 • −12.74 (mean full moon)	

Angular diameter   29.3 to 34.1

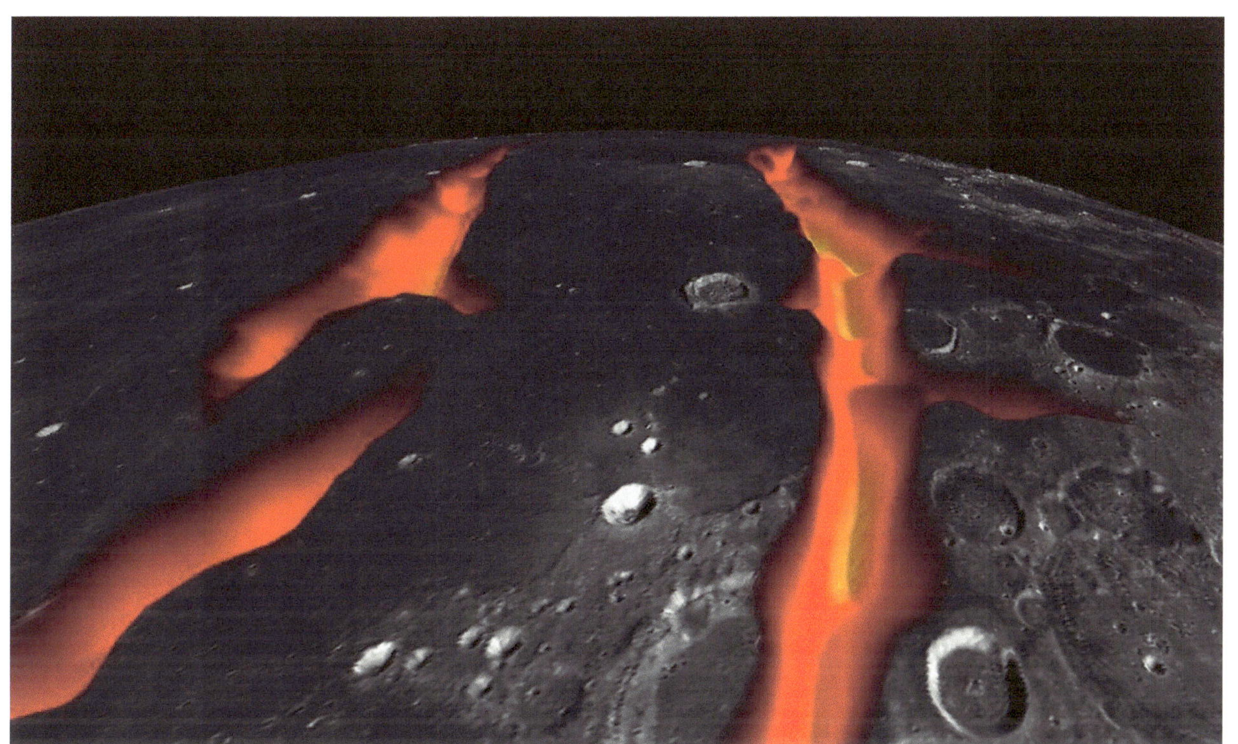

Physical characteristics

Moon is a very slightly scalene ellipsoid due to tidal stretching, with its long axis displaced 30° from facing the Earth (due to gravitational anomalies from impact basins). Its shape is more elongated than current tidal forces can account for. This 'fossil bulge' indicates that the Moon solidified when it orbited at half its current distance to the Earth, and that it is now too cold for its shape to adjust to its orbit.

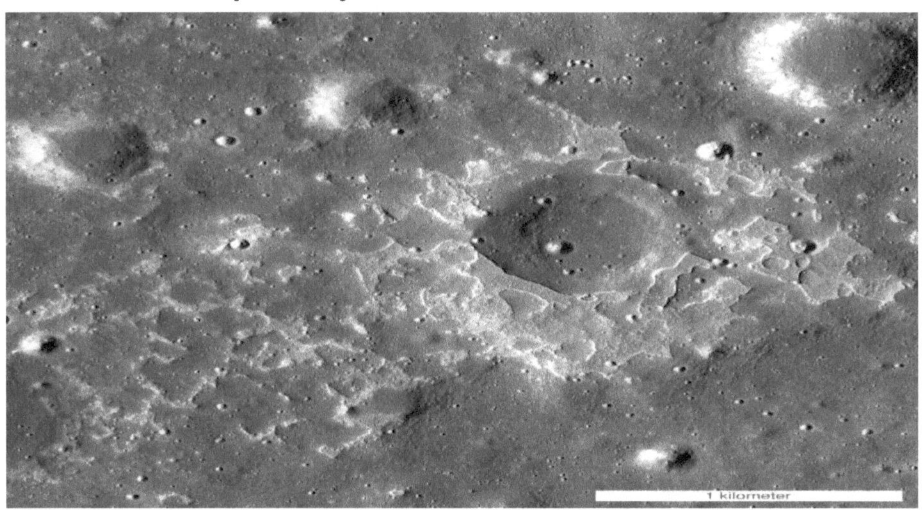

Internal structur

Lunar surface chemical composition

Compound	Formula	Composition	
		Maria	Highlands
silica	SiO_2	45.4%	45.5%
alumina	Al_2O_3	14.9%	24.0%
lime	CaO	11.8%	15.9%
iron(II) oxide	FeO	14.1%	5.9%
magnesia	MgO	9.2%	7.5%
titanium dioxide	TiO_2	3.9%	0.6%
sodium oxide	Na_2O	0.6%	0.6%

The Moon is a differentiated body. It has a geochemically distinct crust, mantle, and core. The Moon has a solid iron-rich inner core with a radius possibly as small as 240 kilometres (150 mi) and a fluid outer core primarily made of liquid iron with a radius of roughly 300 kilometres (190 mi). Around the core is a partially molten boundary layer with a radius of about 500 kilometres (310 mi).

The Moon is the second-densest satellite in the Solar System, after. However, the inner core of the Moon is small, with a radius of about 350 kilometres (220 mi) or less, around 20% of the radius of the Moon. Its composition is not well understood, but is probably metallic iron alloyed with a small amount of sulfur and nickel; analyses of the Moon's time-variable rotation suggest that it is at least partly molten.

Surface geology

The topography of the Moon has been measured with laser altimetry and stereo image analysis. Its most visible topographic feature is the giant far-side South Pole–Aitken basin, some 2,240 km (1,390 mi) in diameter, the largest crater on the Moon and the second-largest confirmed impact crater in the Solar System. At 13 km (8.1 mi) deep, its floor is the lowest point on the surface of the Moon.

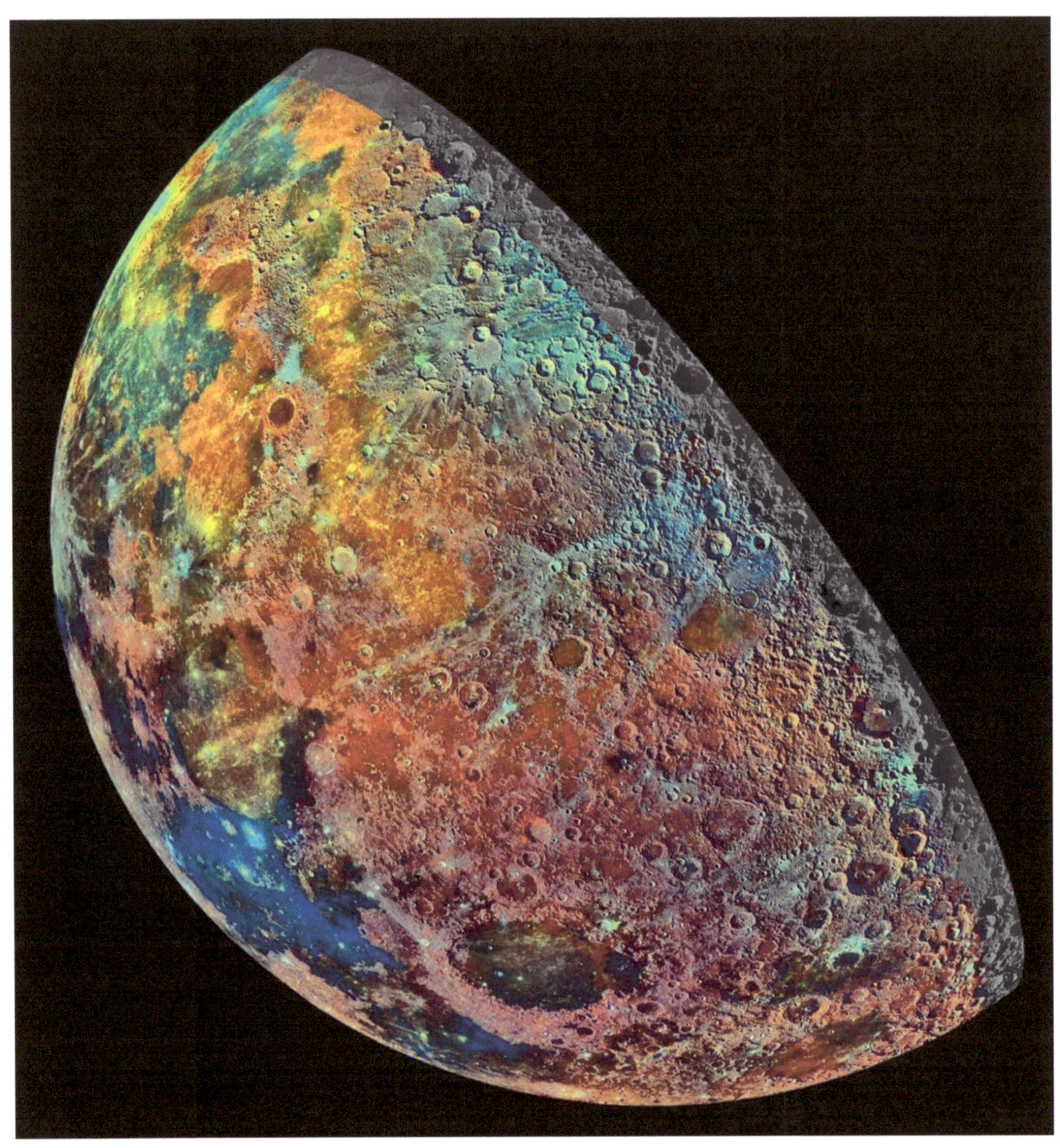

The highest elevations of the surface are located directly to the northeast, and it has been suggested might have been thickened by the oblique formation impact of the South Pole–Aitken basin. Other large impact basins such
as Imbrium, Serenitatis, Crisium, Smythii, **and Orientale also possess regionally low**

elevations and elevated rims. The far side of the lunar surface is on average about 1.9 km (1.2 mi) higher than that of the near side.

The discovery of fault scarp cliffs by the Lunar Reconnaissance Orbiter suggest that the Moon has shrunk within the past billion years, by about 90 metres (300 ft) Similar shrinkage features exist on Mercury. A recent study of over 12000 images

Almost all maria are on the near side of the Moon, and cover 31% of the surface of the near side, compared with 2% of the far side. This is thought to be due to a concentration of heat-producing elements under the crust on the near side, seen on geochemical maps obtained by *Lunar Prospector*'s gamma-ray spectrometer, which would have caused the underlying mantle to heat up, partially melt, rise to the surface and erupt. Most of the Moon's mare basalts erupted during the Imbrian period, 3.0–3.5 billion years ago, although some radiometrically dated samples are as old as 4.2 billion years.

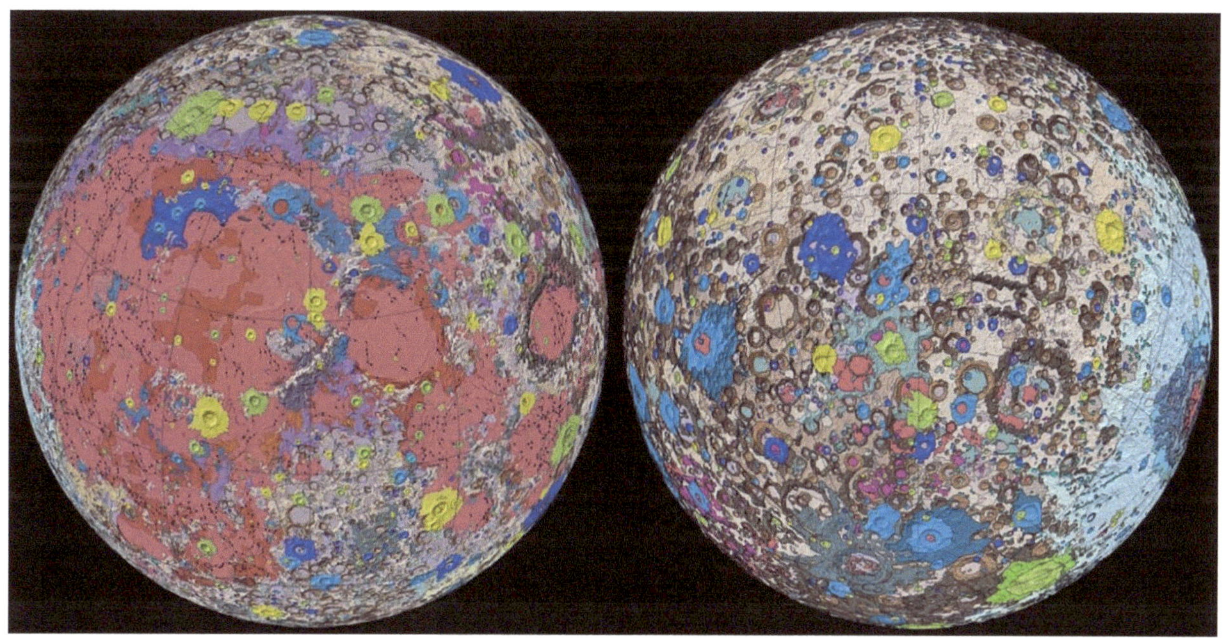

Just prior to this, evidence has been presented for 2–10 million years younger basaltic volcanism inside the crater Lowell, Orientale basin, located in the transition zone between the near and far sides of the Moon. An initially hotter mantle and/or local enrichment of heat-producing elements in the mantle could be responsible for prolonged activities also on the far side in the Orientale basin.

Blanketed on top of the Moon's crust is a highly comminuted (broken into ever smaller particles) and impact gardened surface layer called regolith, formed by impact processes. The finer regolith, the lunar soil of silicon dioxide glass, has a texture resembling snow and a scent resembling spent gunpowder. The regolith of older surfaces is generally thicker than for younger surfaces: it varies in thickness from 10–20 km (6.2–12.4 mi) in the highlands and 3–5 km (1.9–3.1 mi) in the maria. Beneath the finely comminuted regolith layer is the *megaregolith*, a layer of highly fractured bedrock many kilometers thick.

Presence of water

Liquid water cannot persist on the lunar surface. When exposed to solar radiation, water quickly decomposes through a process known as photodissociation and is lost to space. However, since the 1960s, scientists have hypothesized that water ice may be deposited by impacting comets or possibly produced by the reaction of oxygen-rich lunar rocks, and hydrogen from solar wind, leaving traces of water which could possibly persist in cold, permanently shadowed craters at either pole on the Moon. Computer simulations suggest that up to 14,000 km^2 (5,400 sq mi) of the surface may be in permanent shadow. The presence of usable quantities of

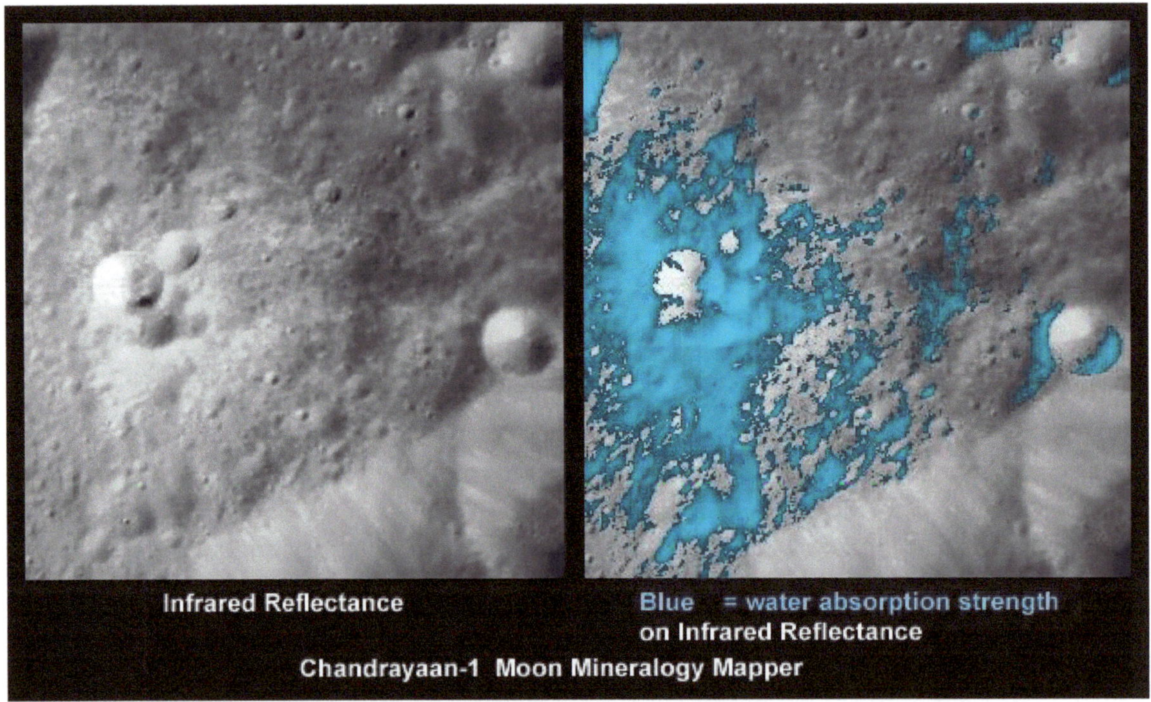

water on the Moon is an important factor in rendering lunar habitation as a cost-effective plan; the alternative of transporting water from Earth would be prohibitively expensive.

In years since, signatures of water have been found to exist on the lunar surface. In 1994, the bistatic radar experiment located on the *Clementine* spacecraft, indicated the existence of small, frozen pockets of water close to the surface. However, later radar observations by Arecibo, suggest these findings may rather be rocks ejected from young impact craters.

The 2008 *Chandrayaan-1* spacecraft has since confirmed the existence of surface water ice, using the on-board Moon Mineralogy Mapper. The spectrometer observed absorption lines common to hydroxyl, in reflected sunlight, providing evidence of large quantities of water ice, on the lunar surface. The spacecraft showed that concentrations may possibly be as high as 1,000 ppm. Using the mapper's reflectance spectra, indirect lighting of areas in shadow confirmed water ice within 20° latitude of both poles in 2018. In 2009, *LCROSS* sent a 2,300 kg (5,100 lb) impactor into a permanently shadowed polar crater, and detected at least 100 kg (220 lb) of water in a plume of ejected material.

Another examination of the LCROSS data showed the amount of detected water to be closer to 155 ± 12 kg (342 ± 26 lb)
In May 2011, 615–1410 ppm water in melt inclusions in lunar sample 74220 was reported, the famous high-titanium "orange glass soil" of volcanic origin collected during the Apollo 17 mission in 1972. The inclusions were formed during explosive eruptions on the Moon approximately 3.7 billion years ago.
In October 2020, astronomers reported detecting molecular water on the sunlit surface of the Moon by several independent spacecraft, including the Stratospheric Observatory for Infrared Astronomy (SOFIA).

Magnetic field

The Moon has an external magnetic field of generally less than 0.2 nanoteslas, or less than one hundred thousandth that of Earth. The Moon does not currently have a global dipolar magnetic field and only has crustal magnetization likely acquired early in its history when a dynamo was still operating, However, early in its history, 4 billion years ago, its magnetic field strength was likely close to that of Earth today. This early dynamo field apparently expired by about one billion years ago, after the lunar core had completely crystallized.

Theoretically, some of the remnant magnetization may originate from transient magnetic fields generated during large impacts through the expansion of plasma clouds The Moon has an atmosphere so tenuous as to be nearly vacuum, with a total mass of less than 10 tonnes (9.8 long tons; 11 short tons) The surface pressure of this small mass is around 3×10^{-15} atm (0.3 nPa); it varies with the lunar day. Its sources include outgassing and sputtering, a product of the bombardment of lunar soil by solar wind ions. Elements that have been detected include sodium and potassium, produced by sputtering (also found in the atmospheres of Mercury and Io); helium-4 and neon from the solar wind; and argon-40, radon-222, and polonium-210, outgassed after their creation by radioactive decay within the crust and mantle.

Past thicker atmosphere

In October 2017, NASA scientists at the Marshall Space Flight Center and the Lunar and Planetary Institute in Houston announced their finding, based on studies of Moon magma samples retrieved by the Apollo missions, that the Moon had once possessed a relatively thick atmosphere for a period of 70 million years between 3 and 4 billion years ago. This atmosphere, sourced from gases ejected from lunar volcanic eruptions, was twice the thickness of that of present-day Mars.

The Moon's axial tilt with respect to the ecliptic is only 1.5424°, much less than the 23.44° of Earth. Because of this, the Moon's solar illumination varies much less with season, and topographical details play a crucial role in seasonal effects. From images taken by *Clementine* in 1994, it appears that four mountainous regions on the rim of the crater Peary at the Moon's north pole may remain illuminated for the entire lunar day, creating peaks of eternal light. No such regions exist at the south pole. Similarly, there are places that remain in permanent shadow at the bottoms of many polar craters, and these "craters of eternal darkness" are extremely cold: *Lunar Reconnaissance Orbiter* measured the lowest summer temperatures in craters at the southern pole at 35 K (−238 °C; −397 °F) and just 26 K (−247 °C; −413 °F) close to the winter solstice in the north polar crater Hermite. This is the coldest temperature in the Solar System ever measured by a spacecraft, colder even than the surface of Pluto .Average temperatures of the Moon's surface are reported, but temperatures of different areas will vary greatly depending upon whether they are in sunlight or shadow.

Rotation

The Moon is rotating around its own axis. This rotation is due to tidal
locking **synchronous to its** orbital period **around Earth.**
The rotation period **depends on the frame of reference. There are sidereal rotation**
periods (or *sidereal day***, in relation to the stars), and synodic rotation periods**
(or *synodic day***, in relation to the Sun). A** lunar day **is a synodic day.**
Because of the tidal locked rotation, the sidereal and synodic rotation periods
correspond to the sidereal (27.3 Earth days) and synodic (29.5 Earth days) orbital
periods.

Human presence

Beside the traces of human activity on the Moon, there have been some intended permanent installations like the *Moon Museum* art piece, Apollo 11 goodwill messages, Lunar plaque, the *Fallen Astronaut* memorial, and other artifacts.

Infrastructure

Longterm missions continuing to be active are some orbiters such as the 2009 launched Lunar Reconnaissance Orbiter surveiling the Moon for future missions, as well as some Landers such as the 2013 launched Chang'e 3 with its Lunar Ultraviolet Telescope still operational.
There are several missions by different agencies and companies planned to establish a longterm human presence on the Moon, with the Lunar Gateway as the currently most advanced project as part of the Artemis program.

Astronomy from the Moon

For many years, the Moon has been recognized as an excellent site for telescopes. It is relatively nearby; astronomical seeing is not a concern; certain craters near the poles are permanently dark and cold, and thus especially useful for infrared telescopes; and radio telescopes on the far side would be shielded from the radio chatter of Earth. The lunar soil, although it poses a problem for any moving parts of telescopes, can be mixed with carbon nanotubes and epoxies and employed in the construction of mirrors up to 50 meters in diameter. A lunar zenith telescope can be made cheaply with an ionic liquid.
In April 1972, the Apollo 16 mission recorded various astronomical photos and spectra in ultraviolet with the Far Ultraviolet Camera/Spectrograph.

Living on the Moon

Humans have stayed for days on the Moon, such as during Apollo 17. One particular challenge for astronauts' daily life during their stay on the surface is the lunar dust sticking to their suits and being carried into their quarters. Subsequently, the dust was tasted and smelled by the astronauts, calling it the

"Apollo aroma". This contamination poses a danger since the fine lunar dust
can cause health issues.
In 2019 at least one plant seed sprouted in an experiment, carried along with other
small life from Earth on the Chang'e 4 lander in its *Lunar Micro Ecosystem*.

Legal status

Although *Luna* landers scattered pennants of the Soviet Union on the Moon, and U.S.
flags were symbolically planted at their landing sites by the Apollo astronauts, no nation
claims ownership of any part of the Moon's surface. Russia, China, India, and the U.S. are
party to the 1967 Outer Space Treaty. which defines the Moon and all outer space as the
"province of all mankind". This treaty also restricts the use of the Moon to peaceful
purposes, explicitly banning military installations and weapons of mass destruction. The
1979 Moon Agreement was created to restrict the exploitation of the Moon's resources by
any single nation, but as of January 2020, it has been signed and ratified by only 18
nations. none of which engages in self-launched human space exploration.

In 2020, U.S. President Donald Trump signed an executive order called
"Encouraging International Support for the Recovery and Use of Space Resources".
The order emphasizes that "the United States does not view outer space as a
'global commons'" and calls the Moon Agreement "a failed attempt at
constraining free enterprise."
The Declaration of the Rights of the Moon was created by a group of independent
researchers in 2021, drawing on precedents in the Rights of Nature movement and
the concept of legal personality for non-human entities in space.

In culture

Mythology

Sun and Moon with faces (1493 woodcut)

The contrast between the brighter highlands and the darker maria creates the patterns seen by different cultures as the Man in the Moon, the rabbit and the buffalo, among others. In many prehistoric and ancient cultures, the Moon was personified as a deity or other supernatural phenomenon, and astrological views of the Moon continue to be propagated today.

In Proto-Indo-European religion, the Moon was personified as the male god *Meh₁not*. The ancient Sumerians believed that the Moon was the god Nanna, who was the father of Inanna, the goddess of the planet Venus, and Utu, the god of the sun. Nanna was later known as Sîn, and was particularly associated with magic and sorcery. In Greco-Roman mythology, the Sun and the Moon are represented as male and female, respectively (Helios/Sol and Selene/Luna), this is a development unique to the eastern Mediterranean and traces of an earlier male moon god in the Greek tradition are preserved in the figure of Menelaus.

In Mesopotamian iconography, the crescent was the primary symbol of Nanna-Sîn. In ancient Greek art, the Moon goddess Selene was represented wearing a crescent on her headgear in an arrangement reminiscent of horns. The star and crescent arrangement also goes back to the Bronze Age, representing either the Sun and Moon, or the Moon and planet Venus, in combination. It came to represent the goddess Artemis or Hecate, and via the patronage of Hecate came to be used as a symbol of Byzantium.

Calendar

The Moon's regular phases make it a very convenient timepiece, and the periods of its waxing and waning form the basis of many of the oldest calendars. Tally sticks, notched bones dating as far back as 20–30,000 years ago, are believed by some to mark the phases of the Moon. The ~30-day month is an approximation of the lunar cycle. The English noun *month* and its cognates in other Germanic languages stem from Proto-Germanic **mænôth-*, which is connected to the above-mentioned Proto-Germanic **mænōn*, indicating the usage of a lunar calendar among the Germanic peoples (Germanic calendar) prior to the adoption of a solar calendar. The PIE root of *moon*, **méh₁nōt*, derives from the PIE verbal root **meh₁-*, "to measure", "indicat[ing] a functional conception of the Moon, i.e. marker of the month" (cf. the English words *measure* and *menstrual*), and echoing the Moon's importance to many ancient cultures in measuring time (see Latin *mensis* and Ancient Greek, meaning "month". Most historical calendars are lunisolar. The 7th-century Islamic calendar is an exceptional example of a purely lunar calendar. Months are traditionally determined by the visual sighting of the hilal, or earliest crescent moon, over the horizon.

Lunar effect

The lunar effect is a purported unproven correlation between specific stages of the roughly 29.5-day lunar cycle and behavior and physiological changes in living beings on Earth, including humans.

The Moon has long been particularly associated with insanity and irrationality; the words *lunacy* and *lunatic* (popular shortening *loony*) are derived from the Latin name for the Moon, *Luna*. Philosophers Aristotle and Pliny the Elder argued that the full moon induced insanity in susceptible individuals, believing that the brain, which is mostly water, must be affected by the Moon and its power over the tides, but the Moon's gravity is too slight to affect any single person.
